Top

100

Poets

100 Winning Poems for a New Century

EDITED BY IAN WALTON

First published in Great Britain in 2000 by
Forward Press
Remus House,
Coltsfoot Drive,
Woodston,
Peterborough, PE2 9JX
Telephone (01733) 898102

SB ISBN 1 86161 781 X

FOREWORD

...far be it from me, or anybody else, to say that one poem is 'better' than another, different maybe - but not better.

THIS IS THE SECOND YEAR of the Forward Press Top 100 poets and the second time the awesome task of 'judging' has fallen to me. Believe me the job is straight out of Room 101.

Presented with thousands of poems, and a strict deadline, and being told, not only to select the 'top' hundred but to then put them into order and award prizes from £50 to £3000 is something of a nightmare.

Had I entered into an intellectual argument with myself: what is poetry, I would still be at it now. So, I focused myself, in the same way as last year and applied the same criteria: content; form; spirit. On first reading, any poem with one of the three properties moved along the desk for a second reading.

A couple of days later I returned to the poems.

The main problem I was facing was my belief that poetry cannot really be competitive. How can a winner be judged. In a fishing competition you just weigh the fish; high jump - did the bar stay up; horse racing - first past the post (with photo-finish to make the difficult decisions). To me, every person that picks up a pen and writes a poem is a winner, and far be it from me, or anybody else, to say that one poem is 'better' than another, different maybe - but not better.

However, I was charged with the task and I embarked on a second reading looking for poems that 'felt' right: the words used, the arrangement and interplay and the extra little something that I cannot put a name to. Eventually I drew out my 100. 100 winners and an office strewn with casualties, each one deserving of a medal.

A few days away from the poems was now a necessity - I had missed the deadline anyway and when I came back to them I felt refreshed.

Choosing seventeen for the major prizes from one hundred was a little easier than choosing the 100.

By this time I had become familiar with them and from the twenty-five I found myself with I gradually moved eight back to 5th position - leaving me my seventeen.

It was only after re-reading and re-reading that, unfortunately, ten poems went in the £100 folder, leaving me with seven, I think, completely different poems.

Seven poems are not too hard to handle - just keep reading them and they will, sort of, select themselves. This may be true but if they put themselves into a different order every day it is not much help. I made the cut and the humour of 'The Americans Stole Our Lunch'; the foggy voice of 'Drifting': the nutty 'Cowboy Genetics' and the sadness of 'September' were my four £250 choices.

On examining my last three (first three really) I could see that for some reason it must have been rhythm that had influenced me most this year.

The 'judging' as I said was a difficult task; signing 100 cheques for 100 poets was a pleasure.

The sensual, if not sexual rhythm of the 'Dancer' by J G Ryder (gender unknown) with the dark finale took a second prize of £500 as did the violent, vicious rhythm of 'Fake It, Break It, Take It, Make It'. Either could have took first prize if the judge's mood had been different that day and if for some reason 'The Last Whale' had not kept swimming to the top.

I was swimming with it, up with the waves for three lines, and down through the surf for one.

So £3000 went to Gary Jeffrey as the 'Last Whale' came first.

Ian Walt

Ian Walton

Editor

The 'judging' as I said was a difficult task; signing 100 cheques for 100 poets was a pleasure.

CONTENTS

5th Prize Winners cont.

5th Prize Winners cont.

The Last Whale

I wish I'd never heard your song
for now its eerie phantom swells
to fill the chambers of my mind
with liquid dizziness.

Your yearning knowing melody
confronts me with its loneliness
and punctuates my consciousness
as if a sound could kill.

The weight of my belated guilt
cries down as crashing waves break through
the brittle surface of the sea
that glimmers with deceit,

as sunlight sinks through solemn eyes
into the ocean's drowning depths
of black and oozing tides that choke
your warnings with contempt.

Directionless migration guides
your grieving song through barren plains
to washed-out shells and shipwrecked bones
that trawl the desert sands.

While empty echoes answer back
your muffled funeral dirge translates
into an ushered hush of myth
lamenting ignorance.

Gary Jeffrey

Fake It, Break It, Take It, Make It

She slashes and crashes her way through the masses:
Devouring, deceiving, moving on.
Then there's a silence, a peace in the violence
Amidst a maddening song.

'I'll deceive if you please
I'll seize what you see,
All is mine to break.
What's done is gone,
Throughout the song
I'm the one who's fake.'

'I fake on him,
I break on her
I take to please my own.'
There's a mouth that breathes
And an eye that sees,
Then wonders at what is shown.

'So slash as I slash
And crash as I crash,
But leave the making to me.
I am not what you are
As you wish on the star,
I am not what before you, you see.'

Debra Lee

The Dancer

Did she notice dark eyes flashing
As she danced by candlelight?
Could she see the wakened passion
Through the darkness of the night?

And the drums beat loud and rhythmic,
Swayed her body to and fro.
While the drums beat loud and rhythmic,
Yet herself she did not know.

Could she sense controlled excitement
As her dance steps out she played?
Did she hear the sighs of pleasure
From her watchers, half afraid?

And the drums beat loud and rhythmic,
Swayed her body to and fro.
While the drums beat loud and rhythmic,
And herself she hated so.

Did she see the looming shadow
Bring the darkened veil of death?
Could she smell the scent of freedom
On the rank and eager breath?

And the drums beat loud and rhythmic,
Swayed her body to and fro.
While the drums beat loud and rhythmic,
Unto death she bade hello.

J G Ryder

The Americans Stole Our Lunch

The Americans bound us in chains,
Tradition has gone to the wall,
They stole our lunch, now all that remains
Is pretty much burger all.

When, back in the early seventies,
Fast food came over the ocean,
Our chance for lunchtime pleasantries
Gave way to time and motion.

Germany too succumbed to the tide,
This couldn't have been expected,
Hamburgers sizzled as onions fried -
Frankfurters too were affected.

The Burghers of Calais were worried,
Not relishing smells from Dover,
Then lost what had once been unhurried
As the take-away took over.

In Europe's South, traditions persist,
They savour their food with pleasure,
I'm sure that they, at least, will resist
And carry on lunching at leisure.

But if ever Spain and Italy fall,
Give way to the fast food trend,
You'll never find lunch in Europe at all -
No starters, no afters, the end.

Steve Woollard

Drifting

You are still drifting
In and out of
My tears
Without warning I find you have
Crept into my mouth and
For a moment we
Feed together from
Mingled juices
And my breath tells truths
Masquerading as lies
Into your neck
And we are only half aware
That there is any
Difference
You are still even now drifting
Through my half-written poems
Which remain forever
Without purpose
Drift with me
For a while through the
Warm-bellied night
If I whisper your name
It is only because
I am
Sleeping.

Moyra Summers

3rd Prize
Winner

Cowboy Genetics

'Yipee-kai-yay' and cry *'Eureka!'*
showdown with the fabric matrix,
no more reason to be weaker
in a tumbleweed of strife.
Let us tinker, let us fiddle,
modify the doggone atoms,
cut the piggy from the middle,
quick draw with the splice of life.

Make it better, make it stronger,
more resilient than coyotes,
make longevity last longer,
kicking nature in the head.
It's darn tootin', keen and peachy,
we're the cowboys of creation,
paraphrasing Friedrich Nietzsche:
'Hasta la vista, God is dead.'

Tony Bush

September

Your face is rain,
I slip into my raincoat
with all the burned
ribbons of summer,
Your love hangs down
into wet trees,
you come from the sky
with a dusty kind
of loneliness,
a stranger walking
me into autumn.

Marion Schoeberlein

Our First Night On Mallorca Island

The island lay sleeping
Under a quilt of nimbus
As we swung in, on a sky
As black as ebony (but for the stars it had snared)

Looking from the window
Like children into a sweet shop
Longing to place toes into
The black, syrup sea.

Touching down, touching hands
Expectant; wearied; awake.
The queue for passports
Like waiting for the guillotine:
It's an old photo; my hair's shorter now.
Just put it in the basket - I'll read it later.

The coach, as old as God.
Over roads like the surface of the moon.
Hoping one of the hotels with a pool
Was ours.

At last. Reception.
Pocket-book Spanish in exchange for the key.
A light switch.
Check the bathroom and the balcony.
Push the beds together.
Time enough to unpack a summer dress, some shorts
Before dinner
Time enough to rip them off again -
To hell with dinner.

Eleven-thirty and barefoot
The sea is warm as blood
The sand is forgiving.
A little smile,
A little sangria,
A lot of kisses.
Our first night on Mallorca Island.

Andrew Detheridge

Postcard From Spain

Light
in duality of wave
and particle
is stable by the laws of
physics.

Wales   .
enduring green and rain
incompatible
is torn and decays from
within.

Spain
exposed to sun-hard heat
deserted lands
that dry to cruel crust
outside.

Words
torment and flay the thoughts hid
by translation
do not conceal the sense
beneath.

So you
and I together in love-tense
duality
maintain a force constant
as stars.

L A Churchill

Stillborn Millennium?

The fire scorched gorse upon the heath bears yet
its buds, vain promises of life to come;
In sepulchres of ghostly white are set
its seeds, now petrified within their womb.
And is the Dome in docklands sterile too,
a barren temple, signifying death
despite bright paint, exhibits rare and new
and sculpted human forms which have no breath
of life? Oh what miscarriage of our pride
that we, in folly, build an empty shell
commemorating years, but not our Guide
the Christ who led us down those years so well.
Great swollen seed pod, London's mighty Dome,
would that you were a birthplace, not a tomb!

Kathy Butler

Another's Cry

Slow motion night when
relentless rhythmic waves
barely parted
the pleasure and the pain
of a new life
flowing in

Same tadpole eyes
and blind snuffling for
the succulent sweetness
he knows is his

Washed up with weariness
I hear another's cry
and in the distance
sea sucks the sand
dry

Julie Brown

Homecoming

He sat at dusk on the outcrop,
black against the grey sky,
sheathed in misery, alone
while rain spat at him, stretching to
touch his ageing face concealed
by the hunch of his shoulders.
So he had sat night after night,
mumbled prayers on his lips,
unaware of the weather that could
not reach him where he sat, immobile,
marked by the torments of time.
Briefly his cigarette glowed,
a spark of red in the night sky,
then as quickly died while
night clouds grew thick around
him, and still he waited,
silent, unmoving in the growing
storm that was not as great as the
one that raged within his heart.
Far off a light shone on the horizon,
looming larger as it took on
shape and form, and somewhere
laughter echoed and a lazy voice
answered in return.
He stood quickly, straining his eyes
out to sea, moonlight turning
his hair to ghostly white.
Shadows of pain vanished, tears
blurred his old eyes and a smile
lingered at his moustached mouth,
his head cocked, listening, watching,
as the fishing boat grated at last onto
silvered sand, dark shapes falling and
tumbling in relief in the moonlight.

Voices greeting, calling, hands slipping
into his, arms of love wrapping him
close to his first born, his son.
Days of torment over, of waiting
and weeping was done, for the great
heaving sea had once again given
him back his son - this time.

Jacki Larcombe

Latex And Leather

She wore latex
He wore leather
Their relationship had no more
commitment than the weather;
and later as years have passed
they still dress up.
Her latex stretched further
over the size of each passing year,
lips still red but the cheeks
no longer hold the blush of youth.
He wears rings
collected over time;
each one holding its own lament.
Still in the bedroom
they chain themselves to what they understand
about each other best,
and something I once would have ridiculed
I now believe is blessed.

R Power

Naked Glass

When the knotted shouts
of woodsmen's throats
are fossilised in the rings of trees.

When a silver fish flicks
from a wave onto soaked sands.

Where the sun shone large
an illumined orange rind
pouring streams of shattered crystal
before the scythe of the bloodshot moon
severed evening
setting its jagged sparks
of naked glass.

Ignas Bednarczyk

Talk Is Cheap

The coffee's still warm
If you'd like us to talk
Do you want to sit here?
We could go for a walk
Upstairs
In your room
The light's fading fast
We're watching the shadows
Unite at long last
To form
One long night together
Forget talk and coffee sips
We can do more than speak
And drink with our lips.

Elizabeth Patterson

At First, No Puffins

At first, no puffins
but a colony of seals, coming home.
Rascally creatures
heads bobbing above the surface
like black footballs,
their side-face white - just for a while
then the ship reversed engines
and pulled away.

In the high-cliffed sea channel
steep-walled
One lone puffin alights on a ledge
just along from dried-up sea pinks.
Its coloured beak overbalancing
and big plastic orange feet.

Sunsparkles dance on the water,
the smell of guano is overpowering
with sounds of birds in galleries.

Out to sea, seals appear
again, playfully teasing
stitching through the waves,
rounded shiny shy needles

Now and then, little black heads appear,
playmates pop up like black commas
punctuating the sea surface.
Then two puffins fly across,
turn and wheel,
these unaerodynamic ice dancers

Past lonely sandy beaches,
it could almost be Greece
but stone is grey instead of white.

June Hogwood

Coffee Morning And Custard Creams

Oh my, my dear,
This reminds me of a childhood fete,
With the tombola,
The treasure hunt,
And the schoolmaster general proud type man,
At the head of the iron gates.

Welcome to the coffee morning darling,
He musters,
Without a shadow of a mutter,
'I like your dress.'
Amiably he speaks,
Thinking that if she was forty years younger he'd have her.
Maybe not,
It's a disgusting thought.
I shouldn't have put it in your respectable head.

I'd like to be there now,
I remember being small and ignored,
All those years ago,
What could I say now to all the gossip
And the purple-tinged perms sipping at an exciting cup of tea,
Because they're somewhere different,
And I suppose they'd better make the most of it,
Before they go back inside,
To stairlifts and all that.

That's what I'd say,
Standing in the way,
Smiling amicably,
Nah, pretentiously.
'Are you going away this year?' they'd ask
I'd reply, meaningfully,

'It's all uncertain yet.'
'Oh,' they'd reply earnestly,
If you could reply earnestly with, 'Oh.'
'Why's that?'
I'd think, then say simply,
'Because I've got Aids.'

And the look of shock on their faces.

Worth a thousand lifetimes.

Anora Kay

Talk To Me

talk to me
I want to watch your lips
and your eyebrows arc when you're mispronouncing a word
talk to me
make yourself heard

talk to me
let me feel that deepest passion
the flicking of your hair when you catch sight of a friend
talk to me
until the end

talk to me
I want to watch you laugh
and notice your nose twitching when you're articulating consonants
talk to me
without hiding your innocence

talk to me
let me hear that singular accent
the gesturing with hands to explain those emotional missions
talk to me
without inhibitions

talk to me
exhale your spirit to meet mine
your eyes express the satisfaction of being listened to
so talk to me
and I'll talk to you

Barry Weldon

Man In The Subway

impoverished
back against the wall
  he sits
    crossed-legged
misery etched on his face
despair in his eyes
hope extinct
quickening footsteps hurry
  past the man
    in the subway
with his back against the wall
head bowed
mumbling to himself
  to anyone who'll listen
    tears glisten
      in the corners of his eyes
thoughts of better days
reduced to begging now
hungry
  no job
    no prospects
      says the card
upon his chest
  who cares
    he's not there
      disillusioned
the man in the subway
with his back against the wall
goes home

Wendy Gledhill

Corpse

The body, they said, would not straighten.
Muscles had contracted, sinews tightened
Until knotted and gnarled. The wound open,
Oozed salt blood that stank and stained the sand.

Washed up like the carcass of some forgotten
Species who had crawled with crippled fingers
Into the unknown, yet we knew you bend
Towards the sea, strong, apart, a stranger.

You left in the early evening dressed in
Your usual way, tight-wrapped, hooded against
The wind to take your walk through the clean
Air which curled round the cliffs near the point.

No more seen alive and no more to see,
The dry salt that caked your black eyelids for days
Was scraped clear in the cold room where we
Were taken apart by your forensic gaze.

The sea returns what it has gathered.
Still it ebbed through your veins breathing water,
Choking your throat, and on your tongue I saw the
Inescapable question of 'Why?' linger.

Death gives no answer, yet somehow our short
History passes in these few moments,
Reveals differences, storms we have fought
And calmed; both of us have clashed against rocks.

On the mantelpiece we have a gilt-framed
Black and white photograph; you by the sea.
My mother gazes at your still flesh and
Her tears soften and straighten your body.

Lawson J Smith

Ferry To An Irish Funeral

The staggering deck
Dips and stomachs us up
Laid between chair legs and tables.
Outside foam heckles the hull
Beneath, monotonous engines
Vibrate, loud as elephants.
A duty-free crowd celebrate:
Perhaps homecoming?
Snuggling close, we try to ignore
The bellowed laughter.
Carpeted steel slams our backs,
Singing, liquid as Guinness,
Lulls us to sleep.

Bleak dawn through Customs
The black of our clothes is a passport.
Then ordering wreathes, drinking tea.
Mourning through a haze of exhaustion.
There was hot soup
After the icy graveyard.
Return was a much calmer crossing.

Lynne Walsh

Only The Ripples Remain

Hapless as a stone thrown
Into a pond
She had gone.
Slipping down out of sight
Into that dread plight
Alzheimer's.

Only the ripples remain
Spreading again and again
Touching more lives with the pain
Of helplessness.

Meg Gilholm

5th Prize
Winner

Hysterectomy

Seventeen months ago she was a young woman;
Her body, a bole of cool marble,
Sculpted,
And scooped away to sweep of limbs,
Polished silken.
Now she is an old woman;
Her flesh a warm corpse
Stinking of stale.

Cut the rose from the root and it withers.
Ineluctable,
Soft folds turn stucco,
Cool skin evaporates to brittle,
Pink wanes,
Fallow,
And perfumes subtle as seasons, pall.

No moon or tide can turn;
Pull back the drag to its moorings.
Her balance is gauntly broken.

I must soar like the eagle now
In desert currents,
Far above your scalpel and your dark heart.

Marilyn Lewis

Song In Spain

I watch the restless sea kiss the soft sand
Laughing in voluptuous play
Smoothing out disquietude
Of walkers' tread the day before.

She sings and dances to amuse her love
She flirts coquettish arms of foam
With salty teardrops to evoke response
From her golden love
She sidles into secret caverns of the bay
Slinking soft against the craggy rocks
Smoothing tenderly to ease her soft self
Into the granite grey limbs.

But then the wind lashes her caress to frenzy
She beats and hurls against the shore
Until the fever dies and she once more
Calmly laps the golden shore.

They are bound forever in peace and tempest
They will never be free from their mutual caress.

Belle Wallace

Three-Part Drama

Scene one; Your shirt needs ironing.
You ask me if I can do it, then
would I like a cup of tea?
I'd like to finish this, but,
you change channels, comment on the news,
and your taste in comedy . . .
Would I like to go out?
(The paint is still wet on the canvas),
I'd like to finish this.
Could I hold your coat while you brush it?
The button is coming loose. Could I sew it on?
The doorbell rings.

Scene two is silence cut through by a siren.
Finding a rose on the doorstep.
The pencil lead broke with the sudden noise.
You propose that we spend the rest of time together.
Your shirts will need ironing.
'I'll do them,' you say.
Cups of tea will have to be made.
'I can do that,' you say.
It's time for another rose and another cup of tea.
I close the door.

Scene three is a blank space.
It is where I breathe in.
Where I rest and where I dream.
It is the journey into myself.
It is me, laughing and dancing.
It is me greeting me,
opening my own doors, letting myself in.

Linda Anne Landers

Chernobyl

In the morning it crackled across the radio
Chernobyl, and a strange yellow light
Filled my mouth with sickness.
That day it rained,
We sludged across the moor, shining orange lamps,
The oilskins smiling water sheets,
Blurs on dead landscape, nothing
But pantaloons of mist, a few crags of deer
Battling away into nowhere. And the rain
Was heavier than ever, and I thought of Noah
And the curved bell of an ark as it came to rest
When the flood was done. But a strange yellow light
Filled my mind that day,
Filled my mouth with rain and crying -
It will not be healed again.

Kenneth C Steven

October

Silence, soft and cool as gentle rain,
falls on paths made dumb by dying leaves,
fills with bronze and gold the firelit lane.
The ragged start of autumn threads and weaves,

twists the frowning edges of the trees,
singes branches later burnt by ice,
a final spark of fire before the freeze.
Leaves scorch on branches tipped with sunset spice,

a blaze of orange darkening to brown;
slow burn of cellulose, receding sap;
hot slips of terracotta floating down.
Nude branches fork like road lines on a map,

no dress of glossy fronds with veins unfurled,
but barren flakes of fire against the cold.
Wisps of dry red leaves with edges curled
change with a silent flame to black leaf mould.

Louise Wilford

Cricket On The Radio

or (Memory of my mother)

England and The West Indies have gone to tea,
But, she continues to garden.
Tractors rumble, bees hum,
Cricket on the radio.
Scruffy black trousers, too big,
Green jumper, too small.
Ebony strands dance into her eyes,
She sweeps them away.

A grumble at the cat.
Waltzing in wellingtons,
Celebrating fallen wickets.

Cut grass and musty pollen
Float on our summer breeze.
A painted memory
In a private gallery.
Loving blue eyes
Creasing into a smile,
As she bends towards her bed of soil.

Elizabeth Everton

5th Prize
Winner

In The Eye Of The Beholder

(For Jenny and Sam)

Yours is not the easy grace of lowland tree,
Whose swaddled seed uncurls its baby root
In sheltered lap,
Whose smooth-barked limbs grow clean and straight
In rippled rings of wood and sap.
No need to question its perfection -
It wears the sun like a jewel.

Your fingers cling to crueller ground -
Granite-gripped, they seek the source
Beneath storm-wrenched gorse and mire.
Each hammered branch and twisted twig
Is wrought in rain and wind and fire,
Whilst lately-budding leaves ignite
In blazing shades of green-drenched light.

Deborah Grashoff

Untitled

Were you there, the time we sailed across a strip
that lead directly above the stars
and into an abyss of planetary bliss?
We flew above technology and below sanity
bordering on an impossible place
where love was love,
place was place,
time was time
and darkness was light.
We rolled in fields of scented blackness
and choked on the dust of life's motorbike.
We danced on the ocean
and loved on a star.
Then to take off again back to life,
back to time, back to place.

D T Morgan

5th Prize
Winner

Sloes

Such jelly we made, that summer you were here!
In jar upon jar we set the Norfolk hours.
A good year that was indeed for sloes .
And all down the sunny meadow-side,
They bowed deeply to our hands, bloom-powdered.

We culled, talked off and on, rejoiced at closeness.
Learning each other as we had not done before.
Our long slow gathering of ripened recognition
Glows in the rich, the jewelled heart of every prim-faced jar,
Blessed with light as a medieval fane.

Mother and daughter, sticky-fingered from the juicy stones,
Aprons stained, hair wispy, we shared the motions of an ancient task,
Mulling our cantlet apples with the sloes
Whose sharpness warmly turned to subtle tang,
Taste of our maturity of loving.

Head bowed by the embrasured window,
You wrote the labels, rueful since you would be far away
When winter breakfasts sang out all our captive summer
And the warming glow of simple loving.

Oh, over there in Oregon, do you remember how we learnt from sloes?

Audrey Capp-Serreau

The Holiday Cottage

The walls whisper of long ago.

Flickering firelit figures dance illuminated on the Yorkshire stone
Like a carousel of an old movie.

Mucky faced children hang around the stairwell.
Tangled hair, like stubble in the summer wind, disguises their features.

He sits with closed eyes, weather-beaten pallor and unshaven chin.
The day's toil done but more to come.

She mends worn rags in the soft candlelight of poverty.
Hacked hands work the needle nimbly.

Dear cottage this was your family of years past.

Then we came.
Pale-faced strangers.
The idle tourists sitting amidst your precious memories.

Some listen and are fortunate to hear your stories.
Told like a parent whose well-loved children have grown up and left
    them in silence.

Sheila Chappell

A Man I Stand

A man I stand within a universe,
Upon a beach, beside the ocean's roar,
Alone you'll find me standing there
And all I carry with me.
Clear blue eyes, wind in my hair,
My blood and bones, complexion fair,
Limbs long and lean to stride the margins of the land,
I stand upon ten million grains of sand.
The heavens are my canopy,
Ten million stars are in the sky,
Each one proclaims my destiny.
A man I stand within a universe,
Integral to a greater plan,
A universe within a man.

Stewart Gordon

Skyscape

To me the sky still seems a holy mystery.
I cannot disassociate myself from hymns
Which sing of spangled heavens, blue celestial light,
Cloud-chariots, glorious rainbows spanning silver space.

I know the moon grows larger as the month proceeds,
And small again after the halfway mark is reached,
But yet I see her as a waxing waning woman,
Clad in thin veils which sometimes hide her changing face.

Fear of flying can be overcome by wonder
At seeing billowy clouds form safety-nets beneath,
But this does not preclude the hope of highest heaven
Far beyond, a gated canopied pearly place.

Science says that planets once were home to life,
While stars are fixed, some only visible through glass;
Poets say the Milky Way leads like a shining road,
Bright constellations are but cloths of five-point lace.

Sunrise paints the air with magic water-colour,
Sunset likewise sweeps his laden brush across massed clouds.
Yes, I must remain with those old music-makers
Who used the skies as confirmation of God's grace.

Mary Hubble

Vanity

Hair hard as cardboard,
Stuck to your scalp,
Face bright and beautiful,
From hours of work,
Clothes firmly pressed,
Dressed to impress,
Smile perfected for a goodnight kiss,
Shoes shiny,
Sparkling in the light,
So happy you could jump,
Spinning head with a whirl,
Boy can be as vain as girl.

Rebecca Bugler (12)

Night Staff

The night is full of breathing without sleep.
Everything breathes,
curtains and lamp and chair,
in rasping, restless movement.
The sly sheet
crumpled with malice
scores my sweating back;
pillows plot to engulf me.
I fight them off
with disobedient, leaden arms,

and then
suddenly
you are there.

The sullen sheet's subdued
and the chastened pillows
resume their rightful role;
the curtain's stilled.
The world is sane once more.
A soft goodnight,
a warm-eyed smile,
and you go down the ward;
the shaded torch
lighting your silent feet.

Now I can sleep
till morning.

Barbara Dickinson

Flower

I sway with the wind
Move fully sideways as I'm not rooted
I give life, though not as freely
Sperm not pollen
My legs give height and strength
As does a stem
My head and face is aesthetic
Just like leaves or petals
My thoughts and opinions hurt
Inside, unlike thorns
I have no roots, just legs
Yet I too decay and die
My seed when sown brings life
That life also requires care
A flower crippled as it knows not its beauty
I'm all too aware of my aesthetics
A flower giving life to others
We only bring death
I am a flower made of flesh
The only difference is I bleed

Kenny Morrison

1913 - 1999

You conducted your death with little fuss or bother,
Fading quietly in to past tense
One unremarkable January night.

We marked the event with a small, grey stone
And the world, barely noticing,
Was subtly changed.

I look for you still, expecting an old man
To be pottering around the garden,
Or laughing so hard you cry.

Drowning in the madness of life,
It was you who sustained my faith
That Goodness can survive.

I lost that one unremarkable January night.

Joanna Day

Senorita Peligrosa

A scorching sun blasts the arena of death
and the voice of civilised man chants
for the queen of the ring to make that final thrust
and bring el toro to his knees.

She twists sensuously
turning this way, then that,
red cape swirling a passionate flamenco
that must end in death.

The bullring queen steps softly
stalking a reluctant foe
and he, now bloodied and weak,
paws the dust in bovine rage
and snorts death to his tormentor.

She wants his ears and tail - the victor's bloody spoils
She craves the adulation of the crowd to feed her massive ego.

He wants her soft belly pinned to his curving horns
and to trample her beneath him.
He yearns to end the piercing agony
and the drug-induced confusion
which clouds his brain.

She struts proud and provocative
the blues and golds of the barbarian's garb glinting in the sun.
With twirling cape she goads the tortured beast
and he turns once more to face her.

His weary head bowed - he charges
hooves pounding to the beat of her heart.
Too late! He swerves and the flash of polished steel
is mirrored in his eyes.

With one lunge the killing blow is struck
and el toro falls defeated at her feet.

Gail McClory

Winifred

Why do you do it,
Winifred?
Why do you stand
Upon your head?
Why don't you stand
Upon your feet,
Like everybody
Else I meet?
Does standing up
That way instead
Ensure you keep
A level head?
Is that the reason
Winifred?

Juliette Matthews (9)

I See You

I see you
You see me
In cellophane
Myth-proof
Mothproof
Dustproof
Reproduction-proof
Not death-proof
Breathing in and out
My own breath
Staring at the world
The world staring back
Dying daily
Until I drop
In my own vacuum
Hermetically, heretically sealed.

Mary Frances Mooney

Darkness

I the bleak nothing,
Visiting the companionless world every night.
I hide auspicious colours,
And straighten all bends.
Dark crippled shapes are made by my body.
Nothing but shadows circle the earth,
Space is everywhere.
Everything I touch or cover
Becomes a dream for many young.
A circular figure turns to a curveless line.
The sun is my enemy the antagonist,
Always making me travel away,
In my hiding place waiting until I swoop back again.

Laura Marples (12)

Youth In Asia

*(Written after watching the media circus surrounding
the Columbine High School shootings)*

When you see the signs in the window,
Does it raise your blood to gun-point?
Crocodile tears for the ratings war:
A sorrow for media's Christ to anoint.
CBS and NBS I'm
Tired 'cause you're just kaffir lovers,
Keep the cameras rolling baby,
15 dead now shoot the others.

Sell your rhetoric on the blood of the fallen,
'Vae Victis' sympathy can't stem this boredom,
Kevin Carter, what was learned?
Kevin Carter, nothing learned.

Will they suffer knee-jerk politics?
Ban handguns now psychos use shotgun.
Now what's the use what's your excuse?
Blame Hitler, Crowley and Manson.
Turn the camera on yourselves,
See alienation in our eyes,
'Has this been coming for some time?'
A fragile breed brought up on your lies.

Sell your rhetoric on the blood of the fallen,
'Vae Victis' sympathy can't stem this boredom
Kevin Carter what was learned?
Kevin Carter nothing learned.

Simon Clay

Alien Ground

After dawn
the thunderfall that
robs the mind
and a looking out of the window
for little things
like spring
that mean nothing
now.

Try not to
remember her
cull the flame
swaying on a wave of hair
the taste of her lips
her skin
and your hands
your strong hands
touching
flying
your groin roaring
for want of her.
Your tears
falling.

Walking over
alien ground
binding broken feet
practising communication
with the living
with the dead
now comes the magic
heart

a voice of love
whispered like
rain in a pool
beneath
the fire.

Squeeze the
butterfly's cocoon
burst the wall
fill the well with sand
the forge is cold
but the iron
fired and deadly
burns.

Winding
the world around his head
taking liberties
with death
a cry in a storm
unheard
kissing the air
with his arms flung out
a man
falls.

Christina Martin

Likor

out of the twin principles of fire and time
a kiss lined with the grime of quicklime and silver likor
i can hear it here, the leeching bleeding
slow tick of clocks and carrion moths
and when it stops

in the tinder of cyrillic lips
it's lost and wasted, purified, nullified   .
fevered, bloody beloved, enraptured in cold panic,
smoke-smothered, the city a sullen flare
in the short distance, dead in air blade-blue

and his taste, my taste in our mouth
sharp and dank, benzine and chemical vodka,
chokes me blind and blank with double tongue
cracking my troubled thunderheads wide open

and the sky is burning through to damned silence
two russian dolls reduced to nuclear ashes

Mandi Kristjen Tweedy

Feminine Is Beautiful

Lipstick traces on cigarettes reflect
explosions, almost amniocentesis, a

release from violence, the frost thawed
from beefed up bones, terse skin, dark

hearts.

Not lily-leaves, pink moons or Ophelia
bathing in the lake, but the staunch stare

of Dietrich, nine year olds in fawn paint
a girl buying a black dress, to become a

woman.

Take me from this tired
male body, I
want to feel warmth

inside. Free me.

Let me run.

James Hulme

The Cuckoo Mistress

*(For all those women who choose to destroy
the love of families, not least their own,
in their need for 'sparkle' through affairs)*

Singular bird,
Swimming in circles,
Darken the skies,
With your sharp spying eyes.

Spying for nests,
Ravenous searching,
Home for the kill,
Moving in for the chill.

Thunderous breaking,
Delicate eggshells,
Twigs laid in love,
Taken captive above.

Dazzled by sparkle,
Collecting the trinkets,
Hiding the brightness,
Gone, the white lightness
          . . . of *truth!*

D Partridge

Remember Abervan

How many others would have come at such short notice, knowing that
Rehearsal of their repertoire would likely be ten minutes flat
We wondered as the choir trooped in all smiles and handshakes,
Greeting us
With confidential murmurings they'd had a practice on the bus.

Maybe we were reminders of a time which had so tragically
Left nothing but despair and shattered dreams within each family
And ever mindful of their loss, they somehow felt they owed a debt
To those bereaved, who like themselves, would take a lifetime to
    forget.

The evening was a great success, the audience response so good
We suddenly became aware that this was something that we should
Repeat each year - they'd been superb -
We booked them in without delay,
To sing at Bishop's Stortford town the following St David's day.

And every year since then they've come,
Like faithful friends, supporting us,
No fee is sought, they even make a quick collection on the bus
To boost the fund which helps safeguard our youngsters' needs,
Attempts to give more quality,
Support and care to how the handicapped must live

And long since then the choir has gone from strength to strength,
Reached high acclaim,
Though this we felt, would not have been, initially their prior aim.
Those men we'd met sang from the soul,
With depth of harmony that rang
Alongside tenderness and pain in memory of Abervan.

Jo Lewis

Sine Qua Non

The stars they shine and light my way
My life if loud, I cannot escape.
I've run so far to find I've begun
The journey back to this thing I abhor.
The screams from Heaven tell me to wrong,
My head and my rhythm, they have grown sore.
Bandage my aches, I can't help myself,
And wound my pain, deliver me to light.
I have arrived, it's time to begin.
Wait for me under the ground,
The quakes will summon us once more.
Rise up to the sun and fight the warring moons,
And remind them of all the hurt they cause themselves.
Then leave them all behind to live or to die as they please.
To begin or to end; yet which is which
This ends, every time.

Danielle Green

Weak

The aching pleasure bursts from her heart,
His faded essence roams the air, and her bed.

The solitary night returns memories, as she would lay,
Rose in hand, naked, silent, less innocent then before.

She had, it seemed, forgotten about the torments
That had made her sob so wildly.

For he did betray her.

She had suffered for what had seemed an eternal youth,
But all of her grief did not quench her fearful thirst
For love from this man.

She was, so I am told, a weak woman.

That's the only thing we share.

Emma Hobden

A Man's Charm - A Woman's Joy

His gentle beauty quickened my heart.
He an angel from heaven torments my sweet nature,
Whose body pleasures me when thrusted on mine.
We are naked, wildly in love; a single beat.
My innocent tongue is now sin.
His tender hands calm my limbs,
And all I feel is his blood boiling through my veins.
I gape at you and see bright stars,
Which run through me like a swift flame of fire.
His essence is mine warmth.
I listen contented to the music you whisper as I fall to sleep,
And wake at the thrill of your breath shadow over me.
I lie awake at night and burst into song,
Till moonlight fills the air with loveliness.
A smile appears as you roam through my mind,
How your memory becomes the reflections of my happiness.
It seems as though you are a form of God,
Too good to be true.
Then your lustre led me astray,
Yet I am not even mad at you.
O I must declare my gratitude I have for you.
You taught me to sacrifice my spirit,
And made me love.
You are neither fierce nor evil.
Though you are my life - my paradise,
The secret to my heart and soul.

Sabeena Jootna

Annunciation

Within her breast she knew
a birth immaculate,
for when gold-white dove flew
she was prepared to wait.

Her guest, bright angel spoke
of interstellar fate:
antique decrees revoke
fresh worlds intoxicate.

The open book refutes
those sects who would debate
the sweet blood-seeded fruits
of ripe pomegranate.

And close by garden wall
three cypresses locate
the hope that stemmed man's fall,
the new life hearts await.

Francis Pettitt

Getting It Together

we are gambling
we are betting
we are beating it all out

just

beating it all out
with

little left for the dry
days.

right now

it all
comes down
on
me

it is raining . . .

there are

pots
frozen chickens

being
tossed around the kitchen

hazel,
this old woman downstairs

is wailing at me, through the din,
her

broomstick urging me for
silence,

i wail back

i'm taking an aspirin

and
she's forgotten

i give her 20 mins resting
time
and
it all begins again

minced meat and
broccoli

B A J Evans

Creation

I'm beginning to feel you inside me
he said, *the simplicity of you,*
the essence of you, the feel of you,
as you are, in me. I knew then
that I had been blurred by his loving,
his unfolding of me, his way of painting
my body, seeing each line, each
curve as if for the first time,
the light of me, the edge of me,
faint sheen of fur which he
loved to nuzzle, cub to lioness.
He played each part of my body
as a musical instrument,
arranging his fingers across my
spine, each knot a key,
my mouth his mouthpiece, playing
the strings of my nerves,
the drum of my pelvic bone. I knew
then that he was creating me anew,
that I was beginning to see myself
as he would have me be.

Teresa Jolly

Reflecting Symmetry

What does it reflect,
the bedroom mirror?
- The symmetrical moons
of your breasts,
and the perfect cleft
of your buttocks,
as you undress -
each curved thigh
a soft mirror to the other,
convexities
and concavities of flesh
leave me spellbound.

Sometimes your striptease
teases me erect,
but tonight,
fatigued,
I bury my face in my pillow -
symmetrically we sink into sleep,
and the body of the bed
swallow us,
whole.

Marc Harris

History

He fought for bones on bended knees
And hunted with the pack.
He learned to kill with hard-strung bow,
And kill his own kind too,
But what no other life-form had
Was thumbs and bright intelligence,
And a need to know it all,
With more aggression than any beast.

Then he was the marching man,
A soldier bound for glory
In every army in the world,
To kill and plunder and to die
In foreign lands so far away,
To make his country proud,
And all for sake of empires great
For emperors and kings.

And next his neighbour became the foe,
He fought for God and State,
For freedom that he never knew,
And never ever would,
Destroying country that he loved
On the rich man's whim,
And died leaving kith and kin
At mercy where none obtained.

So man now at his moral height
Carries bomb and gun,
Distrusting those that share the earth,
Believing nation is at all
And strangers are the foe,
So vandals prowl the world again,
And brave ventures lay in rubble
Still man's against all other men.

Richard Reeve

The Hole

At first a hairline crack across their perfect lawn.
Just the dry weather, they filled it carefully with sand and peat.
A minor irritation, their house and garden were their pride and joy.
The slit grew wider though, a gaping mouth,
Gobbling the crumbling edges, feeding on itself.
On morning, half the manicured grass was gone,
Replaced by deep, dark chasm, sides sliding ominously inwards.
Surveyors and solicitors shook their heads doubtfully.
'Unmarked mine workings, subsidence, slippage,' they muttered.
Lorries rumbled to their door, tipping tons of rubble,
Pouring hard-core into that insatiable maw,
Until its gluttonous appetite was stilled.

Their house and land where they were once so happy,
Has become a place of torment.
They cannot sell it.
Who'd buy a dwelling hollow underneath?
Daily they check their ground and buildings,
For signs of further problems.
This is no act of God, but carelessness by man.
They live tensely on the edge - of the hole.

Peter Hicks

March To The Ark

Today, I drift on a monosyllable
unable to locate the parking slot.
The tide has turned on winter,
still I shiver.

Snow, ice, rain
and more of the same
as oceans swell
to lasso the earth

like a suicide pact
amongst the elements,
raped and maligned
by the carnage of mankind.

The sound of buzzards
wailing in the night,
on untuned ears.
Too deaf to know the harmony of sight.

Stephanie Rankin

The Song Of Concrete In The Rain

Bare trees before the rain-soaked concrete pose,
Point sadly upward to a leaden sky
And shrug their branches as the darkness grows
And hopes of better prospects fade and die.

A symphony of grey on grey unfolds
As murky puddles lurk upon the road;
The glowering sky an inky menace holds
And human faces scowl in sullen mode.

As plodding raindrops slither down the walls
The sodden concrete glares a grim reproach;
On modern buildings deep depression falls,
On people's moods the sorry scenes encroach.

Who says that ugliness is not profound,
A most compelling mystery of its own?
By man's own dullness bleaker Nature's crowned -
There's always one more layer to be shown.

Now winter's grisaille dominates the show,
And taupe and pewter sound the clearest notes;
Today the elements will overflow,
A fact that overwhelming gloom promotes.

The elegiac Muse takes up her lute
To sound the depths of Melancholy's source;
Some say of English weather it's the fruit,
With modern architects to blame, of course.

'Who'd come and live here?' luckless buildings say,
'O hyperactive, we will calm you down.
You need your spirits dampening? We've the way:
In saturated concrete come and drown.'

What metaphors one might see hidden here
Of life's deterioration in our age,
Its many applications all too clear
Satiric inclinations to engage!

Anne Sanderson

Freddie Kruger's Swan Song

It keeps asking questions.
Okay, so no breakfast. Lunch?
Cup of tea (how the donut shop assaulted)

and vitamin C. Hmmph, I'm vegan now.
This afternoon, how liver looks
raw enough to eat while flipping

that phrase like a pancake
cooking on matter turning grey,
seasoned with a hint of self-ingestion:

ripping into dripping flesh
ivory, a mammoth again again again,
consigned to the bowels

of some far-flung corner.
Poor conference, I should've warned him
the horror for a pear on no meat

for, if music be the food of life,
then my stomach claws
Freddie Kruger's swan song!

Sheila Anne Gray

5th Prize
Winner

Birth

In recollection, it is
helium and the legacy
of simpering passion
that leaves no scar
to mark where
soil was scorched
and bones were bleached.

Only the shell of flesh
distended where new life
thrashes and worn life
repairs.

And then, from the union,
the mother, mutant of
fire, struggles naked
and is re-born, screaming
a primal joy.

For the child
is silent; awed, for
the uncompromising sea
has silenced the sands
that bore their footprints.

And that life
unabashed,
forged in the fire,
succoured in the embers,
emerges into the light.

And, in the dawn,
the sky's
swollen womb
smoulders still.

Daphne Gendall

Death Of The Housewife

A tiny tinkle
inside the drum
of the washing machine.
Has somebody's zip bust?
Or was it the chink of glass
against metal
in the memory of the plastic
bowl of washing up?
Did I hear the
sigh of a duster
against the TV screen?
Or perhaps it was
the ghost of
somebody 'being there'
when tradesmen called;
the little woman at
the sink, polishing,
fighting futilely against
hard water deposits.
So where is she now?
Sweeping up the crunchy
specks from glass ceilings?
Or snipping out money-
saving coupons from
knitting magazines?
No, Science has
sucked her down the
sink of oblivion,
pinny and all.
God bless technology!

Sarah Crabtree

1939

Intrigued,
He lifted the file from her desk,
The file she had on him.
The image she wore burned in his mind,
Raven hair, white blouse
Grey professional dress.
If they knew?
If they could see?
How could they, unless . . .
His sweaty hands opened the file
Then with wide eyes he read.
Cold feelings spread,
His nerves cracked like breaking ice.
He only heard a click from behind
And not the trembling finger squeeze the trigger
Or the name she whispered with venom,
'Jew.'

Paul Willis

Wired/Wings

Morning:
Bleak eyes seep silenced words
Broken wings taunt flightless birds
How softly spoken, in jested haste
The blade who enters with fetish taste;
of duck, of chicken, of breast.

Strangers:
Hands which outreach to hold
To be held by anothers muted cold
Of simple screams
and dying dreams;
I wonder aimless in perfection's haze.

Leave:
Sip the ego till the spoon is dry
Splash the tea, make the smudges cry.
Far afield the sun sets golden pearls
In time, close unspoken eyes
To stroke mine beard;
to slowly die.

As you are:
So sullen speech meets with mingled words
And crunching birds grit flightless birds.
Amid an ego that echoes simple screams
and hazy blades to slice bleeding dreams.
Farewell a Princess deep in sleep -
Awake alone
Cuddle your breast;
for it is now yours to keep.

Aka Jazz

Silence Of The Night

I listen to the near silence of the night,
The moon and stars are the only light,
The gentle breeze,
The soft swaying trees,
Silence,
Only broken by the rippling of the stream,
The water, cool, clear and clean,
The sparkling dew on the meadow grass,
Blown by all the winds that pass,
I smell the sweet scent of a red rose,
The wind drops, and no longer blows,
Never have you heard or seen a lovelier sight,
Until you've listened to the near silence of the night.

Jo Bellamy

Twenty Cent Woman

In the brotherhood of man
woman's always been Mother,
Wife, Mistress, Lover or Whore.

She's been property, slave, drudge,
and that old intellectual non starter,
the 'weaker' sex.

But as we have charged
through centuries of ignorance,
prejudice and indifference

woman has moved slowly,
slowly gathering strength.
Now the pace is telling,

the facade is cracking,
and as we're staggering, stumbling
towards a new age woman's passing,

smiling, reaching for the sun.

David Woods

Too Rich

His poetry,
Is too reminiscent,
Of the polar;
Lacks,
That warm breath,
Which cuddles one,
Into life's fertility.

Poetry,
Too rich,
In emptiness;
Could casually,
Lead,
To tendencies,
Sacrificial.

His poetry,
Reeks,
Of abandonment;
Self,
And the world,
At the mercy,
Of profound surrender.

Olando

Whisperings

The wind blew a whisper
Through my part-open door
As if to tell me a secret.
I turned around as if to see the sound.

I turned to see the gentle breeze
Blowing kisses over the trembling trees,
Then dying softly to blow the whispers   .
   towards another day.

I watched it caressing the flowers,
Gathering their scent into a bouquet -
To spread its sweet secret gift
Silently over a waiting world.

What privilege for me, to hear and see
The silent whispers of tranquillity.

Clare Cork

Life Styles

I was born too soon, my mother said
as a young girl, shelling peas.
If they would come without their pods
I'd not waste time on these.

I was born too soon, my father said
as he carved the Sunday joint.
If only it came ready sliced,
then I could see the point.

I was born too soon I often said
as my family I was feeding.
If they'd have pills instead of food
I'd have more time for reading.

I was born just right my brother said
forget that etiquette!
As he watched spacemen suck from tubes
they're not polite, I bet.

I was born too late my daughter said
as she looked at fruit and sighed.
If only I could find some food
not sprayed with pesticide.

I was born too late my grandson cried
only GM food now grows.
With tissue in six-fingered grasp
he wiped his second nose.

Pat Izod

Valerian

Pacific I lie. Surrounded
In black velvet veils, so beautiful
yet in deadly decision he leaves my vessels
empty.
Consummate,
but full of foible. Fatal,
yet invigorating.
A tumult of contradiction
embarks upon a painfully thorny mission
to find truth.
Under thin disguise, yet veiling no fact
and varacity becomes evident.
Ardor. Affection.
He pacifies my thoughts
and soothes my aching mind.
My soporific friend.

Rob Herd

Solitary As An Oyster

Brittle laughter
Breaks the ice-bright air.
Snowflakes, flutter fall, dissolve
On the twitching pond -
Now black glass.

Ducks, swans
Amble, slip, peck absently
At whitened straws of grass.

Daylight ebbs.
A silver moon floats
On an ethereal ocean.

Norwegian Spruce,
Tinsel, designer baubles
Glitter and sparkle.
Candles.
Pristine presents
Port, brandy, sherry.
Chocolates, nuts, cigars, satsumas.
Turkey, thawing slowly.
And a brand new bike
Waiting in the shed
Under heavy tarpaulin.

The moon sails gaily.
An elderly gent stands
Fragile. Forgotten.
Waiting, hoping, thinking
Breathing, seeing, feeling
Blinking, listening, remembering;

Uttering wretched, wasted words.

Deborah L Wilson

Our Mulberry Love

We found each other in our mulberry days
When the blood was meant to be cool and sane.
We laughed and talked . . . grew breathless,
Then recognition suddenly became . . . oh . . . so plain.
Conversation halted . . . our eyes met . . . held . . . we knew,
We had been given something special . . . granted only to the few.
Love, had come to visit a second time;
Life had offered us another chance,
Another bite of the sweet red cherry,
Another tango in the universal dance.
This time the dance wouldn't end till both of us were done;
Dancing into death and eternity,
Forever on and on and on . . .

Valerie Mckinley

Another Look In The Mirror

Guilt is the honour
Bestowed upon man
Describing the error of the reign
As biological guardians
The defenders of faith
The abuse of trust offers shame

Guilty of negligence
A traitor of truth
Flavoured with the taste of deceit
A conceiver of famine
War, death and disease
Furnishing the ecology of earth with conceit

Like a day without sunlight
A night without stars
Like a child without discipline and rule
Mankind stands accused
Of destroying belief
Bearing wisdom while the heart is so cruel

Man lies in a dream
Between darkness and light
Between nihilism and the consummation of life
Between love and hate
In a season of grey
Instigating acts for a self-sacrifice

Time is the observer
The jury and judge
Employing evidence no eyes can deny
Mankind is a plague
A species of death
Another look in the mirror is nigh

David Bridgewater

Brief Summer

Brief summer, must you leave us quite so soon,
Late in arriving, why now haste away?
We'd have you stay with us another moon,
Does autumn's onward march brook no delay?
Alas, 'twould seem this must be so indeed,
For night now steals the minutes from the day,
As summer flowers wilt and cast their seed
And shadows long the sinking sun betray.
Soon will the trees in russet hues appear
And squirrels hide the hazelnuts they find,
Aware, tho' autumn's plenty now is here,
Rude winter's famine lags not far behind.
    We; too, should profit from the changing seasons:
    Nature for their rhythms has her reasons.

Aubrey Woolman

Flight Of Fancy

Standing on the cliff top with my eyes on
the pounding of the sea on rocks below,
dark, angry clouds touching the horizon,
hair getting wet from the first flakes of snow.
The biting wind rushing up the cliff face,
the power of nature filling my mind,
circling me round in its violent embrace,
like kindred elements, two of a kind.
Over the water, my spirit flies high,
divorced from the body, now wild and free,
great flashes of lightning searing the sky,
tempestuous night is now part of me.
My soul travels on, Unknown inviting,
things yet to come, familiar, exciting.

Ann Odger

For Graham

The first moment I saw you at school
I empathised with your loneliness
I was there too; silent screams
and dreams of swinging on shooting stars
were ours, in separate boxes.
As each child turned their back
upon your fumbled speech
I tried to reach your hand with mine
but every time
I failed.

The first time I saw you again
so many years had passed between
so many tears had gone unseen
yet you empathised with my loneliness
you were there too; silent screams
and dreams of marriage and babies
were ours to cast, yet ceased to last
and fell like shooting stars
to a stormy ocean; in slow motion
we failed.

And through it all, you stayed
my closest friend, there to lend
a smile through all the sadness
sanity through all the madness
sweeping away the cobwebs
from my embittered past.
Inferiority complex fading fast;
you helped release my silent screams
yet still our dreams remain
in separate boxes.

Elizabeth Wilson

Undefeated

At the first quick look,
she seemed afraid,
tightly gathered,
propelled to be on guard,
from within her
olive African face.

At the first quick look,
a prisoner of cliché,
I'd wholly missed the defiance
burning through the beauty,
which, at the second quick look,
whooshed over
in deliverance.

African eyes,
young,
still undefeated
in the northern world.

M R Bhagavan

**5th Prize
Winner**

Sleeping

Thief-moon
Pretends to hide
Behind quicksilver edge
Of cloud, sneaks from one
Cloud to the next
Shushing silent stars
That will not betray.
Cold ghost light
Bright through
The night-breath window
Seeks to stir your sleep.
Your sable dreams, the
Frozen smile you wear,
These are not safe.
The cat that the old women
Swear steals children's breath
Pays, purrs body warm.
The Queen of Heaven leaves
No such payment. Daylight
When it comes will wake you.
Lethe-eyed from sleep you
Will not remember how
The Moon, envious
Of your warmth, kissed
You as you slept.

Trevor Smith

Dockland Dusk

Snagged landscape sentences, punctuating black obelisks,
Stretch across a fading image.
Night drops softly in as a pebble falls inside a vast ocean,
Silently.
Old oil, slapped punishingly against piers,
Eddies endlessly in a tidal prison.
Rats stir and begin their dark business,
Secret sampling of human flotsam.
Moored barges rear on the soundless swell
Like dumb, tethered creatures, straining to be free,
And beside them, in miniature imitation, ride wakeful gulls,
Staring into the darkening distance, their thoughts forever
uninterpreted.
Lights stab, showering gold in a radius,
Revealing wind-drifted waste buffeted into deserted doorways.
Waste on waste, lying awry and unaware,
Waste which walks at sunrise.
But until then waits in grotesque petrified parody
To be excavated by tomorrow's driven need.
Dissolving day merges seamlessly into a hundred night-time souls
Who rise, their worship time come,
To praise their shady anonymity,
And wander secure through the snagged landscape sentences.

Jan Crocker

Prince

I looked for you today,
Needing your shoulder to cry on.
I knew where you should be
On a cool, dry day like this.
That sunny spot, sheltered from breezes
By oaks and brambles,
With earth trampled bare by your feet.

You weren't there of course,
How could you be?
I wandered the field, aimless, bereft,
Then stood as you so often did,
With drowsy eyes half closed.

And I could feel the soft smoothness
Of your questing muzzle;
The coarse hair of your mane.
See the burnished chestnut of your summer coat
And smell the sweet breath from your nostrils.

I miss you. Your quiet companionship,
Your unquestioning faithfulness
And your clownish ways.
I miss the freedom you gave me
And the way horizons broadened from your back.

Chris Gutteridge

Judge For Yourself . . .

Surrounded by soldiers He walked,
Along the city streets . . .
While the Jews and the Gentiles talked
Of His wonders and His feats.
And yet these miracles of love
Weren't proof He was divine . . .
To the doubters they weren't enough -
They sought another sign . . .
When Pilate judged that Christ be whipped
And then to set Him free,
The crowd went wild, Christ stood tight-lipped,
Prepared for Calvary.
The Son of God obeyed His Lord,
Through sorrow, pain and strife.
Six hours long His blood outpoured . . .
And then He gave His life . . .
His faithful friends let out a cry
That angels heard in Heaven,
Who knew the reason Christ must die -
For souls to be forgiven!
Within the week God's power came!
The risen Lord lived on!
And in good hearts He lit a flame,
A faith to build upon!
Although Christ died upon the Hill,
He saves lost souls like Saul!
Today, Christ's friends continue still
And preach Good News to all . . .

Denis Martindale

Sleep

Darkest shadows
Sublimed silhouettes.
Parted curtains
Moonshine alley.

Visions stand out
Imagination lingers.
Orbit adventures
In another world.
A revolving kaleidoscope.

Wishes restored on
Unplumped pillows.
Dust on sunlight
Gambols along
The galaxy path.

Turn the cogs
Of the train of life
This morning . . .
another day.

Tim Jellings

Lady Of Boverton

The night air rings
an anniversary,
of fateful love.
Long black hair
trailed forlorn,
catching the winds.
Wept cries hang
like dew, stilled,
upon crumbled ruins.
Banished from the throne,
and he, the King,
of broken vows.
Her heart abolished
thus her soul,
sewn, cloaked,
into seclusion.
Yet her blood craved,
for his warmth.
Her mind in thirst,
for words of love.
And he the adulterer,
had drawn the curtains
of her life.
Feeble arms of milky-white,
clung in anguish.
Revenge, like a line
unwinding, spinning,
in continuation.
Thus her presence
shall multiply,
in armed mutiny!
For wherever the King
may wander,
may his conscience
break into fragments.
And may he taste
the plight,
of his guilt
every time! Forever more!

Amanda Jane Martin

In Truth

Sometimes I dream I can build castles,
But in truth I can only gather stones.

Sometimes I dream I can compose symphonies,
But in truth I can only create noise.

Sometimes I dream I can write poems,
But in truth I can only scribble words.

In truth, all I can do is dream,
But in dreaming I can do all I wish to do.

David Rhine

The News

I sat upon a sandy beach
And turned my back to the sun.
Minutes before I had been
Basking in the beauty of existence,
Imagining a world far beyond reality
And revelling in the simpleness of it all.
Now, this memory was tainted.
Before I heard the news I had passed
Through the sandy street, working
My way towards a busy taverna.
Crowds of strangers shadowing a
Foreign television set. The Greek
Words flittered past my ears and
I supped on my soup. Then I heard
Her name and it all began to fall
Into place. A crash, a death, several
Deaths. A world a million miles away
From my own, mourned a Princess.
Yet I sat in the shade of the sun, in
Paradise. Confusion, guilt perhaps
That I had not appreciated her life
Whilst she still had it. A stranger to
Myself, yet a reality. I turned my
Back on the crowds and slowly
Walked towards the beach, my feet
Hardly touching the ground. The sun
Scorched my shoulders and brought
Tears to my eyes. I watched the faces
Of strangers as I passed them, children
Full of life. I smiled.

Elisabeth Abby Godfrey

Spring Cleaning

Winter snarls 'Silence!' with an edict cold,
and strips the trees to bony-fingered grief,
with scarce one desperate leaflet to enfold,
their naked poverty.

Spring smiles and draws the curtains of the dawn,
washes the woods and hills with April showers,
lays fresh green sheets on Mother Nature's bed,
and carpets her home with rainbows of vernal flowers,
as cuckoo pipes 'Reveille!'

Betty Gardner

Unfading Years

When I must leave
I will take within my hands
some pebbles burnished bright
by the ceaseless
washing of the sea,
and in the other,
lift from gleaming
of golden sands,
a few minute
and shaded shells,
shaped and curved
by centuries of time.

I will hide them
in some secret place,
in pools of tears, and rain
that even falls in city streets,
and in this broken shrine
of memory, to touch
the reflected beauty
of all those treasured things
so loved
in those unfading years.

Jean Mary Orr

Intangible

I fell in love with a face on a leaf
through a window

It turned to smile and beckon in the sultry gale

so timid was my sense of touch
I shied away - behind the frame

as my fingers   .
- blistering with the needs for words

mimicked to the vision a makeshift kiss

felt the complexion of the leaf
and embraced bliss.

Sebastian Pengoir

The Scents Of Rain

O closing midnight of your fall -
Moon drifted, a breathless shroud,
Silent snowfall,
Gathering its mantis-prey.
You.
My valuable, unrequited.

Fluent sea swarmed at your door;
It needed you.
Like me.
Like cigarettes.

You were hunter and the hunted.

I crave you, umbilicus;
You were the shine in the studying eye.
A gymnasium of muscles smiling.

I praised you with a hooded kiss -
Elated - I left your very door
For whatever makes you happy . . .

The scents of rain,
Drizzling column of stars,
Crackled at your wake.
The ferryman left you beneath
A sea of plasma, penniless.
I could not swim -
You drowning, stillborn.
My heart's blood pooled like distant tears.

Now the status of goddess is in you . . .

The ones we miss
Tend the warm flocks of mortal earth.
Living in poetry, we meet.

Julian Allard

Innocent As Doves, But Wise As Serpents
(Matthew 10:16)

Our law is their law, so it does not matter how
Our consciences dictate; there is no escape now.
Come in all you others with lifestyles so deviant;
We must appear fair and in your sins be compliant.

Read this pornography, my dear pure infant;
For this type of literature I have to be tolerant.
The days are here when I'm not allowed to guide you.
My soul, no longer my own, is controlled by the EU.

I have spoken before of my views on abortion,
But now I must be quiet and speak with great caution.
At pointed hats and magic spells I heartily laughed
But now I must change my views to encompass witchcraft.

We've cast off the years taken to mould democratic freedom;
Replaced with European Superstate instead of United Kingdom.
Pray hard, dear Christians, we've become a sect as predicted.
We will find that our personal liberties will now be restricted.

The battle with Mammon to keep Sunday special was lost.
Pray to stay British or our country will soon count the cost.
Pray that in our lifestyles we'll be innocent as doves,
Or do you accept we can have all sorts of strange loves?

Ask God to help our fellow Europeans to live a Christian life,
Safe from one where homosexuality, witchcraft and abortions are rife.
We still show naiveté in our churches and government to date.
We urgently need the wisdom of serpents before it's too late.

Wendy A Nottingham

Plant A Tree For Me

(Dedicated to Martin, my grandson)

'Alas poor Freda!
A cardboard box, not a brass-handled coffin
No marble headstone, not cremated'
Teenaged grandson, (stomach orientated)
'Let's plant a cherry tree, or pear
Then there's something to eat when we visit there'

No choir, nor campanologists ringing
I'm planted where the birds are singing
In a beautiful wildflower parkland
With deer grazing there, close at hand
No more bills to pay, no noise, at least
Surroundings here of perfect peace

Far from the rat-race and pollution
Putting me here is the best solution
An amateur poet - though no Laureate
In this resting place some peace I'll get
No horse-drawn drays, or long black hearses
Now, no deadline dates to compose my verses

Freda Baxter

Strange Way To Start A Revolution

A half-heard conversation - the strangest
basis for theology that I can
imagine.

The weaknesses of the West:
a single voice of protest taking stand,
'I'm sorry, I don't agree,' undermines
its own authority. Better than true
tyranny? Perhaps. (In my soundest mind
I can charitably extol virtues
of otherwise natural enemies.)

Still I find it strange that private letters
should define us, with all their might have beens,
what ifs and buts, and hands of editors.
Apollos' appeals? Unheard, unwritten.
In such manner is the Lord's word given.

Dyfrig Lewis

Totality

Clouds loomed menacingly
over St Michael's Mount
charcoal-leaden, wispy, several shades of grey
watery sun peeked through preparing
to encounter a lesser light
Rain fell in a veil of tears
a Hercules ascended high till it
was way above the cimbrus clouds;
It was ten-fifty; cameras poised for action
as time ticked tantalisingly slow . . .

11am.
and the moon bit the orange
like a hungry dragon devouring its prey
the world was stationary
and the dent deepened into solar golden glow
everything turned a whiter shade of grey
a hushed dusk fell; darkness deepened
This was the moment.
Somewhere a beaked Concorde took flight
Like a big blanket an ethereal gloom enveloped
everyone, (even Patrick Moore)
Stonehenge stood in stark silence
as Druids danced
gannets retreated to rocky roosts
the sun succumbed to lunar light
in this, the twilight hour . . .

Moon moved onwards, ever on
till Bailey's bright beads appeared
and a huge diamond ring shone sparkling
in a near high noon.

Somewhere a Concorde chased a shadowed sun
being followed by a full moon shadow.

Judy Studd

To Dr MMK

(A connoisseur of observed inappropriate behaviour)

Brolly furled and smartly suited
Show your ticket, swiftly footed
Squash in train, sit thigh to thigh,
Never catch another's eye.

The two hour trip in company
Should bring familiarity
But
The only talk that's ever done
Is loudly on a mobile phone.

'I'm on the train! It's running late!
My drink and dinner have to wait!'
A man of great pomposity
Spewing forth inanity.

Such a buzz of conversation,
Each wrapped up in isolation.
Man must make his greatness known
By public use of mobile phone.

Carol Morris

Colouring

Grandad you taught me
with bright felt tips,
to colour with care
around the edges
of my picture.

The perfectionist,
you gave up,
before I could prove to you
my life was good.

Surrounded
by your paintings,
I wanted to tell you that
we were your creation,
the achievement you longed for.

Quietly, slowly
you let your whistle fade.
Brushes, paints, pastels,
pinks, reds, yellows
tidied neatly away
in shoeboxes.

You sat in your chair,
lifeless
in life.
So it seemed to me
you sat and waited for the end.

But the children
of your life,
we live on,
Colouring boldly, brightly but carefully.

Suzann Taylor

Loose Ends

I start, but I cannot finish.
In my wake hang the pale ghosts of
conversations, relationships,
near-friendships and good intentions
all unresolved.

My bedroom desk - its drawers packed
full of notebooks, their pages crammed
with stories, all going nowhere;
with nice first lines, but no poems
to follow on.

Declarations of love to a
strange girl are met with approval,
but boldness dies. I avoid her,
shying away, knowing her name
but nothing more.

The ticking bomb undelivered,
just dropped off in any old place
to slice with shrapnel fresh green lives
which end, in knee-deep pools of gore,
far too early.

The child conceived, then aborted;
the well-prepared speech, killed by nerves;
the bridge collapsing in mid-storm -
such is the way with one who starts,
but cannot fin

Richard Fallis

Emily Bronte

They wrap you up like a
Bronte biscuit
And keep you in the box
Marked *Do Not Touch*
But you slip through the
Intellectual's net
You with your obnoxious
Foot-stamp
And your temper rising
Like the bread you baked
So passionately
And when your bossy
Older sister lifted the
Lid on Pandora's Box
And spied your rhymes
And declared your
Insolent genius open
To the world
I would have given anything
To have been a silent fly
On the wall observing
Your calm handling of the situation . . .
Mystic visionary
Bog-hopping over Haworth Moor
In a Laura Ashley nightie?
No you were too human
The god of visions did not
Reject you
Being loved senseless
And returning the passion
This was how God made you
And this absence claimed you.

Sharon Marshall

Rebirth

I was a shell
just waiting to hatch.

Hoping to feel whole;
for the smelting
to be complete.

To find myself
in a bed of roses
awakening in my coffin
clawing to safety.

The cocoon had long since rotted away

And so it begins
as finally the temperature sets
and the shell cracks

Hollow.

I'm beginning to discover myself,
to realise what is inside.
The shell is breaking, its hollowness –
once a quality –
disappearing beneath the light
fading to grey.

The transformation beginning
I'm emerging – as years of uncertainty are melting.

The focus shifts –
the dead emotions
remain in the wooden box.

The settling; the butterfly wings

The colours of life
twinkling, beginning to spark
to sparkle and grow

No more depression, no more fear
the nemesis is burning.

A new chapter, a new wright

A new poem.

Duncan Campbell

You Throw Fish

You have my attention
for what it's worth - have it.
Caught in the tow of your net
dragged through grey water
for the sake of being wrong
just one fish amongst many,
another wriggler.

On your pillow
like a dark, bottomless well
your tears of thirteen years
have filled the space
so you can shed revenge
on unsuspecting suitors.

You throw fish into the sea
and cast your net again
wider, further, faster,
braving the strongest gale
and the roughest wave.

But we fish learn fast
and have dodged your trawler
finding better plates to adorn
more tender bites to endure.

Andy McPheat

Lady

Sometimes
Her heart would break
Like iron oxide cloud busts,
Across a feathered sky.
For love is a hurting thing
Throwing into heavenly chaos,
All that it holds within. ·
Bringing only
A blush of rose rush memories
Before,
Her sun sailed by.

Tonight
She would wear a moon face
And not forgetting,
A dress of forest green.
Bringing
The scent of shaded bluebells
Into his heart to stay,
Where once
Only her love had been.

Across a darkened room
She will reach him,
Just as the music plays low.
Holding the last dance
Of burnt sienna stars in her eyes
Before,
She finally lets him go.

Norman Royal

INFORMATION

We hope you have enjoyed reading this book - and
that you will continue to enjoy it in the coming years.

If you would like to enter this year's competition then
drop us a line, or give us a call, and we'll send you a
free information pack.

Contact :-
Forward Press Top 100 Information
Remus House
Coltsfoot Drive
Woodston
Peterborough
PE2 9JX
Tel: (01733) 898102
Fax: (01733) 313524